10 TIPS TO STEP -

PARENTING

CONNIE ALSOBROOK

This book is dedicated to anyone that grew up with a step – parent. Some of us had great step-parents and some of us did not. We know the challenges of trying to fit in an already made family or maybe a step-parent that did not have any children. We learned first hand what and what not to do with step-children we may be blessed with one day.

Preface

Having been inspired to help alleviate the issues associated with step-parenting, I've put enough time into studying and understanding how step-parenting related issues can be solved. I came up with this book "10 steps to step-parenting," this book shows the closeness and the authority to discipline step-child develops over time, and neither should be rushed. For example, step-parents are often eager to build a relationship, and they commonly seek one-on-one activities with step-children. But for a time, step-children are often uncomfortable being alone with a step-parent.

Immediately the remarriage takes place, the most successful stepparent-stepchild relationships are those where the step-parent focuses first on the development of a warm and friendly interaction style with the step- child. Once a foundation of mutual respect and affection is established, step-parents who attempt to assume a disciplinarian role are less likely to be met with resentment from the step-child. After a period of time, one-on-one opportunities are received more openly. The length of time required for step-children to build a relationship with their step-parent depends on a number of factors. This is why it's so important to let the step- child set the pace for their relationship with you. Nonetheless, the book is also admonishing you as step- parent to learn about the child's interests, meet them where they are, never exclude them, and speak only positive words to them.

One of the most important step-parenting skills after remarriage is to never compare your children to your step-children. Comparison between these two can bring about disparity and enmity. Avoid comparing your step- children with your children, or addressing them as your step-children to outsiders. Also, biological parents need to remain the primary caregivers and disciplinarians. Handing off the children to the new step-parent sabotages his or her ability to build a relationship with them, because this can cause unforeseen enmity. Step parents need to grow into their relationship with their step-children. Be friendly at first, and support the house's rules. Seek to be mutually close to your step- children, and enjoy the relationship you have with them. Let the children set the pace for their relationship with you as their step-parent. Consider each child in all of your decisions. Give and expect affection, nurturance, and emotional closeness only to the degree your step- children appear comfortable with. As you go ahead with the "10 steps to step-parenting," you'll realize what you may have been getting wrong as a step-parent, and how you can get it right, which is my aim for this book.

Parenting is a fluid experience, and there is no single solution to all the issues that are faced daily when it comes to raising kids. Nonetheless, it is especially trickier when you are raising step-children. However, there are tips you can follow in order to have a healthy family…..but nothing is 100% guaranteed.

1. Don't force anything

Always understand that you can't force the children to like you. Acknowledging their presence and how important they are to the family may be all they need to come around and feel comfortable with you. Rushing children will appear fake and insincere. So, let things take their natural course and be patient.

"Peace cannot be kept by force;
it can only be achieved by understanding."
Albert Einstein

2.   Let them know the door is always open for conversations

Be approachable and let them know they can come to you with any problems they are having at any point. Don't scold them for every little issue. Instead, let them know of other options they could have chosen. Too much repriminding can drive them away from you and from discussing important matters with you.

Open the door of your heart with the hands of love, and you will realize how beautiful the whole universe is!

Namita Sirdesshpande

3.   Meet them where they are.

Try to see things from their perspective. Meet them where they are or meet them halfway and come to an agreement that works for both of you, not neglecting the fact that you are still the adult.

"Don't push people to where you want to be; meet them where they are."

Meghan Keaney Anderson

4.   Never exclude them.

All the children in the house should have the same choices and opportunities. If one child does not receive something and the other does, let it be for a legitimate reason. Explain to the child why they were not able to get the same item. Examples: Age appropriate, child is on punishment, allergies, fear, not interested, etc. Don't keep them out of discussions that concern them directly or indirectly. Let them have a say in some things that pertain to their future. This will show them how much you value their opinion.

Negative is born in the gap where love has been excluded.

Deepak Chopra

5.   Speak only positive words to them.

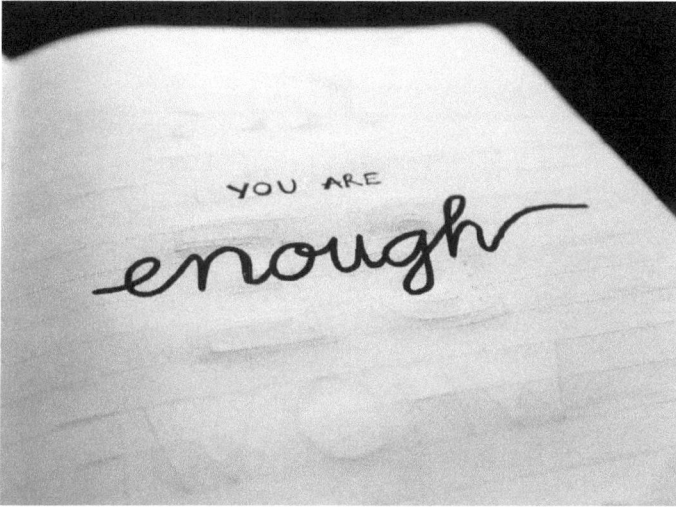

There is a lot of power in positive affirmations, and you must speak these positive words to them consistently. When you speak positivity to your children, they become more confident in themselves. This will help them to start looking at situations with a positive attitude, making them more optimistic. Negative words can last a lifetime, causing problems well into their adult life.

Reach high, for stars lie hidden in your soul. Dream deep, for every dream precedes the goal.

Pamela Vaull Starr

6.   Never refer to them as your step-children.

Stating that "these are your children and these are my step-kids" in public automatically allows people and your step children know you see them differently. You should not say such things unless you are asked directly. If you are ever asked about your step children, speak about how blessed you are to have them and how they are no different from if you had given birth to them yourself. Children remember things like this and take them to heart, it is hurtful to separate your biological kids from your step-children in front of others.

Step parents are around to add to a child's life not to replace the biological parent.

Connie Alsobrook

7. Don't snitch on your step-children.

Nobody likes a snitch. Try to resolve the small issues you observe with them. Don't go telling your spouse every time something comes up, making your spouse out to be the villain. This can make children resent their own parent, which can cause them to dislike you because it now seems like you have turned their biological parent against them.

Honestly it's never about the surface issues,

its about the unsaid issues that frustrate and hurt us.

Connie Alsobrook

8. Do not talk negatively about the child's biological parent, and do not co-sign if your spouse does.

This is a huge no. It is not fair to speak ill of a parent that is not present to defend himself/herself. In addition, it is not a step-parent's place to plant negative seeds into a child's mind and heart. If there is nothing positive to say, keep your mouth closed, especially when the child is present. You may not think a child is listening, but they usually are.

If someone speak badly of others, the negative energy that put out into the universe, will return to same person. The same is true of positive energy Now choices are yours!!!

Mrityunjay Kumar

9. Never compare your children and your step-children.

Comparison is at the root of dissatisfaction, and you must never compare your kids with any other kid. What's even worse than comparing your kids to outsiders is comparing them with your step-children. This will create unwanted enmity between them, and this is far from ideal. Your house will always be divided, and a divided home will never have peace.

Comparison is the most poisonous element in the human heart because it destroys ingenuity and it robs peace and joy"

Euginia Herlihy

10. Don't make your spouse (biological parent) be the bad person.

Don't try to paint your spouse as the bad person by making them always discipline the children. Resist the urge to blame your spouse or make them look bad in front of your kids. A typical example of this would be telling them to punish your step-child and you pretend you have no knowledge of the situation. Making them feel like they are choosing the step-parent over their child. This is similar to snitching......

You never look good trying to make someone else look bad Unkown

With these few tips, you have a simple guide of the dos and don'ts of raising step-children. It doesn't matter if they are your biological children, or step-kids. In the end, they are kids, and you must be sensitive to their needs.

Children are a gift and should be treated as such.

Connie Alsobrook

PROOF

www.ingramcontent.com/pod-product-compliance
Lightning Source LLC
Chambersburg PA
CBHW040347060426
42445CB00029B/30